Sports Illustrated KIDS

W9-BLP-342

Strength Training
for Teen Athletes
Exercises to Take Your Game to the Next Level

by Karen Latchana Kenney

Consultant:
Thomas Inkrott
Head Strength and Conditioning Coach
Minnesota State University, Mankato

CAPSTONE PRESS
a capstone imprint

APR 2 3 2012

Sports Illustrated Kids Sports Training Zone is published by Capstone Press,
1710 Roe Crest Drive, North Mankato, Minnesota 56003.
www.capstonepress.com

Books published by Capstone Press are manufactured with paper
containing at least 10 percent post-consumer waste.

Library of Congress Cataloging-in-Publication Data
Kenney, Karen Latchana.
  Strength training for teen athletes : exercises to take your game to the next level /
by Karen Latchana Kenney.
     p. cm.—(Sports illustrated kids. sports training zone.)
  Includes bibliographical references and index.
  ISBN 978-1-4296-7680-9 (library binding)
  ISBN 978-1-4296-8002-8 (paperback)
  1. Teenage athletes—Training of—Juvenile literature. 2. Muscle strength—Juvenile
literature. I. Title. II. Series.
  GV711.5.K455 2012
  613.711—dc23   2011033561

Editorial Credits
Anthony Wacholtz, editor; Heidi Thompson, designer; Eric Gohl, media researcher;
    Marcy Morin, scheduler; Laura Manthe, production specialist

Photo Credits
TJ Thoraldson Digital Photography, all interior training photos

iStockphoto: Prokhorov, design element (backgrounds); Sports Illustrated: Al Tielemans,
back cover, 17, Bob Martin, cover (bottom right), Chuck Solomon, cover (top), Damian
Strohmeyer, (bottom middle right), 26, John Biever, cover, 4, John W. McDonough, cover
(bottom middle left), 5, Peter Read Miller, cover (bottom middle), 16, 27, Robert Beck,
36–37, Simon Bruty, cover (bottom left), 6–7

Printed in the United States of America in North Mankato, Minnesota.
102011   006405CGS12

TABLE of CONTENTS

WHAT IS
Strength
Training?

Can you kick a soccer ball across the field? Can you dunk a basketball? Can you smash a baseball over the fence? Strength is behind your kick, jump, and swing power. Strength is needed in every sport. Your strength not only helps you perform better, but it also can keep injuries to a minimum.

MLB FIRST BASEMAN
MIGUEL CABRERA

Are You Ready?

Your power is located in your muscles. Strength training uses resistance to build your muscles. Resistance can come from your own body's weight or certain training tools. When you do a push-up, you use body weight to build your muscles. Rubber cords and elastic bands stretch to make resistance. Heavy medicine balls and weights can be lifted and moved. Weight machines are usually found in gyms. They are used to work certain muscles. Stability balls can also be used in exercises to work muscles harder.

EXERCISES ARE OFTEN DONE IN SETS, WITH A NUMBER OF **REPETITIONS**, OR REPS IN EACH SET. BE SURE TO PACE YOURSELF BY RESTING FOR ONE OR TWO MINUTES BETWEEN EACH SET.

When you strength train, you do exercises that work various muscles in your body. You can focus on one muscle area, such as your legs. Or you can work your whole body with exercises that are good for every muscle group. Whatever exercises you choose to do, write them down. This is your training program. You can look at it while you are training to help you remember what exercises to do. It should also list each exercise's number of repetitions.

At your training sessions, don't forget to warm up and cool down. To warm up, you should jog in place or do jumping jacks to get your muscles ready to train. It can also prevent you from hurting your muscles. You should stretch your muscles when you cool down. This step will keep your muscles from cramping and leaving you sore.

Now that you know the basics, it's time to start training! Pick the exercises that will help you in your sport. Work on your shoulders to help your basketball pass. Make your chest muscles stronger to improve your swimming stroke. Soon you'll feel your hard work pay off as your strength grows.

WNBA STAR
SEIMONE AUGUSTUS

FACT: Be sure to include a proper warm-up and cool down for your workout.
- Warm up: 10–15 minutes
- Strength train: 20–30 minutes
- Cool down: 10–15 minutes

STANCE—ANY FORCE THAT SLOWS OR STOPS MOVEMENT OF THE BODY
TITIONS—THE NUMBER OF TIMES AN EXERCISE IS DONE

Hard Hits, Powerful Swings

Tackling players on a football field takes incredible arm strength. So does swinging a bat or a tennis racket. Whether you're on baseball or softball fields or the tennis court, balls won't go very far without some power behind your hit.

This striking action is used in hockey and golf too. Swimmers need powerful arms and shoulders for good arm strokes. And what about volleyball? It takes strength to serve and pass. Work on your arms and shoulders. These exercises will increase their strength.

SHOULDER ROTATIONS

2 OR 3 SETS OF 10–15 REPS

Shoulder rotation exercises strengthen the muscles surrounding the shoulder joint. Your shoulder rotates at the joint to perform a range of movements. Try this exercise to keep your shoulders and arms moving smoothly and strongly.

WHAT YOU'LL NEED

- exercise mat
- hand weights
- towel or pillow (optional)

1. Lay your mat on the ground. Lie on your back. You can use a towel or pillow to support your head.

2. Grab a hand weight in each hand. Your lower arms should point toward the ceiling. Make sure your elbows touch the floor during the entire exercise.

3. Slowly move your lower arms in the direction of your head. Stop once you feel resistance. Then bring your arms back so your hands point to the ceiling again.

TIP:

Remember to start small with your weights. Using weights that are too heavy may cause damage to your shoulders. Three-pound weights work best for this exercise.

4. Slowly move your lower arms so they point toward your hips. Stop once you feel resistance. Then return your arms to the starting position.

Keep Your Balance

When strength training, you should equally work both sides of your body or muscle group. For example, it's important to work both the internal and external muscles of the shoulder. This keeps your muscle strength balanced. Every person has two sets of muscle groups in their bodies—one on each side. Some muscle groups also have two sides. If one side is weaker than the other, injuries are more likely to occur. The weaker muscle is worked too hard and can become sore. To prevent injuries, do equal repetitions of exercises using the same amount of weight on both sides of the body.

SEATED SHOULDER PRESS

2 OR 3 SETS OF 10–15 REPS

You'll feel this exercise work your deltoids. These muscles are right above your shoulder joints. Working them will strengthen your shoulders and increase your lifting power.

WHAT YOU'LL NEED

• rubber cord with handles

1. Hold one handle of the rubber cord in each hand. Sit on the middle of the rubber cord on the ground. Keep your back straight by tightening your stomach muscles.

2. Put your elbows at shoulder height. Face your palms forward.

TIP:

Remember to breathe! Exhale slowly when you lift your arms. Then inhale slowly when you lower your arms.

3. Stretch the cord by slowly pushing your arms up. Keep pushing until your arms are straight above your shoulders.

4. Lower your arms slowly until your elbows are at shoulder height. Repeat the exercise.

VARIATION

To mix it up, try alternating arms. Push your left arm up until it is straight above your left shoulder. Slowly lower your arm to the starting position. Then do the same for your right arm. Alternate arms until you've finished the reps.

DELTOIDS—THE TRIANGLE-SHAPED MUSCLES COVERING THE SHOULDER JOINT

TRICEPS PRESS

2 OR 3 SETS OF 8–12 REPS — — — — — — — —

The **triceps** are muscles you use to extend your arms. Strong triceps make for a better throw, whether it's shooting hoops or performing a soccer throw-in.

WHAT YOU'LL NEED

• medicine ball

1. Stand with your feet as wide apart as your hips. Keep your back straight. Hold the medicine ball in your hands.

2. Raise your arms up and bend them backward. The medicine ball will be behind your head. This is your starting position.

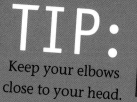

TIP:
Keep your elbows
close to your head.

3. Lift the ball over your
head until your arms are
straight. Keep your elbows
and upper arms still.

4. Lower the ball back to
the starting position.
Then repeat the exercise.

VARIATION

YOU CAN ALSO DO THE TRICEPS PRESS FROM A
SEATED POSITION. REMEMBER TO KEEP YOUR BACK
STRAIGHT DURING THE EXERCISE. ANY WORKOUT
BENCH WILL WORK, BUT IT'S BEST TO USE ONE
THAT HAS A BACK SUPPORT.

Keep at It!

You may not notice if you are getting
stronger right away. But with regular
training, small changes happen every
day. Don't give up! It may take some
time, but you will start to see the
difference in your strength.

TRICEPS—THE LARGE MUSCLES AT THE BACK OF YOUR UPPER ARMS

HAMMER CURL

2 OR 3 SETS OF 8–12 REPS

This exercise is great for your **biceps**. These muscles help your shoulders and elbows and are used for almost every arm movement. Keeping your biceps strong will help your arms stay in top shape.

WHAT YOU'LL NEED

• two hand weights

1. Grab a hand weight in each hand. Stand with your back straight and your feet as wide as your hips. Slightly bend your knees.

2. Place your hands by your thighs with your palms facing your body.

BICEPS—THE LARGE MUSCLES AT THE FRONT OF THE UPPER ARMS

TIP:
Keep your back straight and your elbows locked against your body. Standing against a wall can help you keep your back straight.

3. Now bend your arms at your elbows. Move your hands up toward your shoulders. Count to three while moving your arms. At three, the weights should be by your shoulders.

Don't Forget to Rest!

Wait a day between strength training sessions. It will give your muscles a break. Working them too hard may cause injuries. It might also keep you on the bench during the next big game.

4. Now move your hands slowly back down to your thighs. Repeat the exercise.

VARIATION

You can alternate arms while doing hammer curls. Do a hammer curl with one arm, then switch to the other. You should do the same number of reps for each arm as you would for the regular hammer curls.

Building Power from the Core

What's your core? It's the middle of your body, where strength moves from your legs and hips up to your arms and shoulders. Your **abdominals**, **obliques**, and lower back are the muscle areas of the core. The power to hit a baseball or softball starts in the legs and hips. Without a strong core, power can't pass to the arms to make the hit.

ABDOMINALS—THE MUSCLES AT THE FRONT OF THE BODY BY THE STOMACH
OBLIQUES—THE MUSCLES AT THE SIDES OF THE BODY NEAR THE STOMACH

It's the same for tennis, lacrosse, and football players. They need a strong core to hit or pass balls or make a tackle. Train your core and you'll feel the strength in all your movements.

THE PLANK

2 OR 3 SETS OF 15–20 SECONDS AND WORK YOUR WAY UP TO 1–2 MINUTES

The plank focuses on your abdominals, hips, and back. Hold the plank position for as long as you can. Each time you try it, your core will get stronger.

WHAT YOU'LL NEED

• floor mat

1. Lie face down on the mat. Your arms should be underneath you.

2. Lift up so your elbows are at 90-degree angles.

TIP:

Your back may start sagging toward the floor during this exercise. If it does, just tighten your abdominals to push your back to a straight position.

3. Lift your body up onto your toes and keep your lower arms on the mat. Keep your body straight and your stomach muscles tight.

4. Hold this position for as long as possible. Count out loud and see what number you reach before stopping. Try for a longer time during your next workout.

All about Form

Having the right form is critical in certain strength training exercises. Your form is the shape of your body while doing an exercise. If you do a dead lift with poor form, you may injure your back. To watch your form, try exercising in a room with mirrors on a wall. Or watch someone who is experienced doing the exercise to study his or her form. To reduce your risk of injury, try the exercise a few times without weights. Study your form to make sure it is right. Then add weights to the exercise.

BALL CRUNCH

2 OR 3 SETS OF 10–25 REPS

It takes some balance to complete these crunches. Using a stability ball is a little tricky, but it helps your abdominals get a great workout.

WHAT YOU'LL NEED

- stability ball

Lay back onto a stability ball. Make sure it supports your lower back. Keep your feet on the ground and your knees at a 90-degree angle. Put your hands across your chest.

2. Raise your upper body toward your knees.

3. Hold your position for a few seconds. Then slide back to your starting position and repeat the crunch.

VARIATION

TO MAKE THE CRUNCH HARDER, PUT YOUR HANDS BEHIND YOUR HEAD.

TIP:

Move your feet wider apart on the floor to help keep your balance. Do this exercise slowly. If you go too fast, you may fall off the ball.

THE BACK BEND

2 OR 3 SETS OF 8–15 REPS — — — — — — — — —

A back bend works your core, but it's also a great stretch. It's a small movement, but you can feel it from your neck down to your abdominals. Strengthen your back with this exercise.

WHAT YOU'LL NEED

• floor mat

1. Lie face down on a floor mat. Clasp your hands behind your head.

2. Tighten your stomach muscles and place your chin on the mat.

3. Lift your **torso** off the mat as far as you can. Hold your position for a few seconds. If you need help keeping your lower body on the mat, ask a friend to press down on your thighs.

4. Slowly lower your torso back down to the mat.

A Tougher Back Bend

You can also do a back bend starting in a standing position. On a soft surface, stand with your legs shoulder-width apart with your arms above your head. Slowly bend your back and lower yourself backward until your hands reach the floor. If it's your first time performing a back bend, use a wall to catch yourself. After you get the hang of it, move away from the wall a little and try it again. Eventually you will be far enough away from the wall so that your hands will reach the floor.

TORSO—THE UPPER PART OF THE BODY, NOT INCLUDING THE HEAD AND ARMS

SINGLE-LEG SQUAT

2 OR 3 SETS OF 8–10 REPS

It's a balancing act to perform this exercise correctly. After a few reps, you will feel the burn in your abdominals, quadriceps, hamstrings, and gluteus muscles.

1. Stand with both feet hip-width apart on the floor. Bend your knees and tighten your stomach muscles.

2. Place your arms out in front of you. Raise one foot slightly from the ground.

3. Sit back to do the squat. Do not let your knee bend past your toes.

4. Slowly straighten your leg again to stand back up. Repeat 10 times squatting on the same leg.

5. Repeat the squats with the other leg.

TIP:

If you're having trouble keeping your balance, hold on to something sturdy with one hand.

QUADRICEPS—THE LARGE MUSCLE AT THE FRONT OF THE THIGH USED TO EXTEND THE LEG

GLUTEUS—THE MUSCLE ON THE BUTTOCKS THAT MOVES THE THIGHS

A Push for Upper-Body Power

Good defensive players need chest strength on the football field. They constantly push and block the other team's players. Pushing strength comes from the chest muscles and moves out to the arms. Quarterbacks also need strong chests to throw the ball down the field. Speed comes from chest strength for swimmers and rowers. It's necessary for a good breaststroke or freestyle. Baseball and softball players use this muscle group too. The muscles make pitches faster and swings stronger.

BENCH PRESS

2 OR 3 SETS OF 8–12 REPS

The bench press is a powerful exercise that works both your chest and arms. Athletes from almost any sport can benefit from the bench press.

WHAT YOU'LL NEED

- raised bench
- two hand weights

1. Lay with your back flat on a bench. Place your head on the bench. Keep your feet on the ground as far out as your shoulders. Hold a weight in each hand.

2. Stretch your arms up so the weights are above your chest. Your hands should face your feet.

3. Slowly lower each hand weight. Stop when your triceps are parallel to the floor.

4. Raise your arms slowly back above your chest.

Spotters

A spotter is someone who stands by while you are doing an exercise. The spotter can help you if a weight becomes too heavy. If you are doing an exercise the wrong way, your spotter can tell you how to do it the right way. Ask someone to spot you if you are just starting out with weights or beginning to use heavier weights.

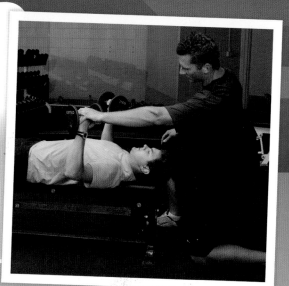

PUSH-UPS

2 OR 3 SETS OF 5–20 REPS

This classic exercise is great for strengthening your chest and arm muscles. Once you get the hang of it, increase your repetitions. You'll soon notice the difference.

1. Lie with your face down on the floor. Place your hands a little wider apart than your shoulders on the floor.

2. Lift your body up so that you are on your hands and toes. Keep your body flat and your arms straight.

3. Slowly lower your upper body to the floor. Bend your elbows until your chest almost touches the floor.

4. Push back up with your arms until they are straight again.

VARIATION

YOU CAN ALSO TRY A STANDING PUSH-UP. PROP YOURSELF UP AGAINST A WALL WITH YOUR ARMS EXTENDED AND YOUR HANDS AT SHOULDER HEIGHT. SLOWLY BEND YOUR ARMS UNTIL YOUR FACE IS CLOSE TO THE WALL. THEN PUSH OUT UNTIL YOUR ARMS ARE STRAIGHT AGAIN.

Progression

As you continue training, add more weight and repetitions to keep the workout challenging. Increasing weights and repetitions is called progression. It's best to progress slowly. Add more repetitions after you've been doing an exercise for several weeks. If you are doing 10 push-ups for a few weeks, add five or 10 more for the next few weeks. Doing too much too soon will only hurt your muscles. You'll know that you are using too much weight if you can't do an exercise the correct way. Go slowly and you'll get long-lasting results.

MEDICINE
BALL PUSH

2 OR 3 SETS OF 5–10 REPS

The pushing action used in this exercise is especially great for basketball and volleyball training. It works both the chest and the arms while testing your reaction time.

WHAT YOU'LL NEED

- rubber medicine ball
- space to move around

1. On a hard floor, stand with your feet shoulder-width apart. Bend your knees slightly.

2. Hold the medicine ball by your chest with both hands.

3. Push the ball down as hard as you can. Let it drop to the floor and bounce.

4. Catch the ball after it bounces. Then repeat the exercise.

TIP:

Watch out! Don't let the medicine ball hit your face when it bounces back up. Throw it forward a little so it bounces up at an angle.

33

CHEST PRESS

THREE SETS OF 10–20 REPS – – – – – – – – – – – –

This chest exercise can be done anywhere as long as you have a stability ball. The chest press is a simple exercise that works both your arms and chest.

WHAT YOU'LL NEED

- rubber cord
- stability ball

1. Wrap the rubber cord around your back. Hold a handle in each hand. Your feet should be shoulder-width apart.

2. With your elbows bent, place your hands by your chest. Face your palms down. Sit on the stability ball.

3. Slowly straighten your arms, pushing out from your chest.

4. Return to your starting position.

Ouch! That Hurts!

Sometimes injuries can happen during a workout. You might work a muscle too hard. You could also slip and fall while doing an exercise. If you feel any pain or hear a pop during your training session, stop what you're doing. Let an adult know right away. To help prevent an injury, follow a few simple steps:

- Make sure you know the right way to do an exercise before beginning it. Ask a friend or an adult to help you the first few times if you are unsure.
- Don't push yourself too hard or too fast. Do a small number of repetitions at first. Then each week add a few more.
- Wear the right clothing. Athletic shoes grip the floor well. Comfortable, well-fitting clothes help you move more easily.

Run Faster, Jump Higher

What do basketball and volleyball have in common? You need to jump! And jumping takes strength in your legs and hips. Without it, you won't get very high. Your legs and hips also help you run fast, stop and turn, and kick. That's great for athletes in soccer, lacrosse, football, rugby, and many more sports. These exercises will work out your leg and hip muscles.

BRAZILIAN OLYMPIC
VOLLEYBALL PLAYERS
WALEWSKA OLIVEIRA (LEFT)
AND HÉLIA (FOFÃO) SOUZA

U.S. Olympic volleyball player Kimberly Glass

DUMBBELL SQUAT

2 OR 3 SETS OF 8–10 REPS

Squats are great exercises for working your entire leg, from your hips down to your toes. Start with small weights at first. Then increase them as you become more confident doing this exercise.

WHAT YOU'LL NEED

- two hand weights
- room to move

1. Hold a weight in each hand with your palms facing your body. Stand with your feet as wide as your hips. Slightly point your toes away from your body.

2. Sit back while bending your knees. Stop when your thighs are parallel to the floor. Keep your arms pointing toward the floor, your back straight, and your head facing forward. Keep your heels on the ground.

3. Slowly straighten your legs and knees to stand again.

Be Careful!

Many people mistakenly bend forward while doing squats. Don't do this! Remember to sit back as if you are sitting in a chair.

TIP:

Don't let your knees go too far forward. If they go past your toes, that's too far.

90-DEGREE JUMPS

2 OR 3 OF 4–12 REPS—START WITH 4 REPS AND WORK YOUR WAY UP

Ninety-degree jumps are not only a good exercise to increase your strength, but they also are a good **anaerobic exercise**. It can be hard to keep your balance, but remember to stay focused while jumping. This exercise will definitely help on the basketball court.

WHAT YOU'LL NEED

• space to jump

1 Stand facing forward with your feet as wide apart as your hips.

ANAEROBIC EXERCISE—A TYPE OF EXERCISE THAT YOUR MUSCLES DON'T NEED OXYGEN TO PERFORM

2. Bend your knees and jump as high as you can. While in the air, turn your body 90 degrees to the right.

TIP:

Swing your arms when you jump. You'll jump even higher!

3. Jump again while turning 90 degrees to the left. You will face your starting point when you land.

So Sore!

It's pretty common to feel sore after you train your muscles. When you start to work out, your muscles aren't used to all the activity. They are worked harder than they are used to being worked. This damages the muscles a little, which makes them sore. Don't worry. Your muscles heal and grow stronger after each workout. If they are really sore, use an ice pack on the sore spot. And don't forget to rest a day or two between workouts.

4. Repeat the exercise by starting with a 90-degree jump to the left.

LEG CURLS

2 OR 3 SETS OF 8–12 REPS

Leg curls work your hamstrings. Your hamstring muscles are used when you bend your knee and extend your leg. This helps you walk, run, jump, and climb. Try these curls to keep your hamstrings strong.

WHAT YOU'LL NEED

- rubber cord with handles
- chair

1. Put one handle of the cord through the other handle. This makes a large loop.

2. Slip the loop around your right ankle. Then step on the cord with your left foot. Hang onto a chair with your left hand.

3. Bend your right leg up, and then lower your leg. Complete your repetitions for the right leg.

4. Switch the loop to your left leg. Step on the cord with your right foot. Then do the same number of curls using the left leg.

Stay Hydrated

Drink water while you train. You lose water by sweating when you exercise. If you drink plenty of water, you will feel less tired from your workout.

POWER LUNGES

2 OR 3 SETS OF 4–7 REPS PER LEG

It takes balance to do a power lunge. You might be a bit wobbly at first. But keep trying. You'll soon notice your upper legs getting stronger.

WHAT YOU'LL NEED

- space to move
- two hand weights

1. Stand with your feet as wide apart as your hips. Hold a hand weight in each hand and face forward.

TIP:

You can injure yourself if you let your knee extend past your foot. It puts too much pressure on your knee. Make sure your knee never extends past your ankle.

2. Take a big step forward with your left foot. Bend your knee and lower your body until your thigh is parallel with the floor. Make sure your knee lines up with your ankle.

3. Push off the floor with your left foot. Return to a standing position.

4. Repeat the exercise with your right foot and leg.

STRENGTH TRAINING IS A TYPE OF EXERCISE THAT TAKES TIME TO SEE RESULTS. BE PATIENT WHILE TRAINING. WORK THE SAME MUSCLE GROUPS WHILE SLOWLY INCREASING YOUR REPETITIONS AND WEIGHTS. REMEMBER TO REST BETWEEN WORKOUTS. WITH REGULAR TRAINING, YOU WILL BEGIN TO SEE RESULTS. YOUR MUSCLES WILL LOOK MORE TONED AND YOUR STRENGTH WILL INCREASE. YOU'LL HAVE MORE STRENGTH BEHIND EVERY GOAL-SCORING SOCCER KICK, VOLLEYBALL JUMP SERVE, AND BASEBALL OR SOFTBALL SWING. SO KEEP UP THE TRAINING AND GET IN THE GAME!

Glossary

abdominals—the muscles below the chest in the stomach area; also called abs

anaerobic exercise—a type of exercise that the muscles don't need oxygen to perform

balanced—when the two sides of a person's body or muscle group have equal strength and size

biceps—the large muscles at the front of the upper arms

deltoids—the triangle-shaped muscles covering the shoulder joint; deltoids are used to raise your arms away from your body

gluteus—the muscle on the buttocks that moves the thighs

hamstrings—the muscles at the back of the upper leg; hamstrings allow the legs to flex and extend

obliques—side abdominal muscles that help you bend and rotate your torso

parallel—an equal distance apart; two straight lines that are parallel will always stay the same distance from each other and never meet

quadriceps—the large muscle at the front of the thigh used to extend the leg

repetitions—the number of times an exercise is done in a set; also called reps

resistance—any force that slows or stops movement of the body; when used in training, muscles work harder to push against the resistance

torso—the upper part of the body, not including the head and arms

triceps—the large muscles at the back of the upper arms

Read More

Mason, Paul. *Improving Strength and Power.* Training for Sports. New York: PowerKids Press, 2011.

Payment, Simone. *What Happens to Your Body When You Run.* The How and Why of Exercise. New York: Rosen Central, 2010.

Shaffer, Alyssa. *Feeling Great: A Girl's Guide to Fitness, Friends & Fun.* Middleton, Wis. American Girl Publishing, 2010.

St. Germain, Wendy. *Talking about Exercise.* Healthy Living. New York: Gareth Stevens Pub., 2010.

Internet Sites

FactHound offers a safe, fun way to find Internet sites related to this book. All of the sites on FactHound have been researched by our staff.

Here's all you do:

Visit *www.facthound.com*

Type in this code: 9781429676809

Index